THE YOUNG
SCREENWRITER'S GUIDE

THE YOUNG SCREENWRITER'S GUIDE

EDWARD SANTIAGO

ARCHWAY
PUBLISHING

This book is a work of non-fiction. Unless otherwise noted, the author and the publisher make no explicit guarantees as to the accuracy of the information contained in this book and in some cases, names of people and places have been altered to protect their privacy.

Archway Publishing books may be ordered through booksellers or by contacting:

Archway Publishing
1663 Liberty Drive
Bloomington, IN 47403
www.archwaypublishing.com
844-669-3957

Because of the dynamic nature of the Internet, any web addresses or links contained in this book may have changed since publication and may no longer be valid. The views expressed in this work are solely those of the author and do not necessarily reflect the views of the publisher, and the publisher hereby disclaims any responsibility for them.

Interior Image Credit: Alba Peña

ISBN: 978-1-6657-5505-4 (sc)
ISBN: 978-1-6657-5506-1 (e)

Library of Congress Control Number: 2024900528

Print information available on the last page.

Archway Publishing rev. date: 01/10/2024

This book was written on a
1956 Smith-Corona Silent Super
typewriter machine and
edited on a 2020 Apple M1
Mac mini.

In loving memory of
Hipólito and Lydia Santiago

I wish you could have seen this.

I wish…

CONTENTS

ACKNOWLEDGMENTS

I wish to thank the following people who, one way or another, helped make this book possible with their suggestions, ideas, and encouragement: My brothers Alex, Bob, and Jose Santiago for being there in good and hard times. The Peña family: Ameli, Monica, Adelita, and especially Irene Peña, for liking this book and my award-winning script *Knights of the Valiant Heart.* My dear friends Sue Smith, Vanessa Ionta Wright, Arika F. Cullen, Wilfred Esteves, Yarim Machado, Frank Montalvo, Caroline Lake, Kerri Lynn Dee, Val Valdez, and Barbara King for your input and encouragement. Faiza Kracheni, the staff, and my Austin School of Film students. Sally Vidal, whose input as an educator was vital at the beginning of this project. Olga Edmé Rivera-Ramos, thank you for being my teacher and friend. Your impact on my life has been invaluable.

Alba Peña, you found me at the lowest point in my life. Thanks to your love and for believing in me; you made me a better man.

Last but not least, thank you, young screenwriter, for writing the new movies that will entertain us.

INTRODUCTION

Welcome, young screenwriter! This guide is created to introduce you to the basics of screenwriting. The basics of screenwriting, or movie writing, are easy to learn, yet they will take time to master.

For a while now, I wanted to create a screenwriting book for younger adults. I've been teaching adult students the art of scriptwriting since 2016 and realized there are few resources for young writers. Screenwriting shouldn't be limited to the older demographic when people of any age can do it with the correct know-how. We're all innate storytellers; some develop this ability to the fullest. If you have an idea you want to see made into a movie, then this is the book to guide you, young screenwriter.

This book will introduce you to concepts like the *three-act structure*, the elements of the script, and other screenwriting concepts to provide you with the necessary skills to write your first short film script.

TOOLS OF THE TRADE

To write screenplays, you'll need a few essential tools. Here are a few tools that will make it easier to write your script:

1. Pen and notebook: Many screenwriters prefer to write their first draft script in an 8.5" x 11" notebook. They place the elements of the script (see Chapter 2) in the correct position on the page. Later, they transcribed it to the computer using screenwriting software.

2. Index cards: 3" x 5" cards are great for writing down individual scenes when outlining your script.

3. iPad or Android tablet: With Bluetooth technology, you can connect a keyboard and mouse to an iPad or Android device, using them like mini laptop computers. There are also screenwriting apps like Final Draft for iOS.

4. Mac or PC computers: If you have access to a Mac or PC, many software suites are available for different budgets. The advantage of using software apps is that they can make it easier to set the correct formatting for screenwriting instead of manually formatting in Word or Pages. Here's a list of a few of the many apps available:
    *   Final Draft (www.finaldraft.com)
    *   SoCreate (www.socreate.it)
    *   Fade In (www.fadeinpro.com)
    *   Celtx (www.celtx.com)
    *   WriterDuet (www.writerduet.com)

5. Typewriter: Typewriters are machines that were very popular during the twentieth century. They were used for writing letters, books, and even screenplays. They are hard to find, but many antique sellers have them available. This book was written using a 1956 Smith-Corona Silent Super typewriter machine. If you find one, try it. The experience is unique and magical.

WHAT IS A STORY?

People have told stories since ancient times across many generations and civilizations. Thanks to these stories, we know of many heroes who inspire and entertain us. Old heroes like Hercules, Perseus, Robin Hood, King Arthur, and many others have paved the way for modern heroes like Superman, Optimus Prime, and Harry Potter, among countless others.

Of course, what are heroes without their adventures? Heroes face challenges and perils alongside their companions and allies who clash against their opposition: villains and henchmen who battle our heroes in an exciting conflict that entertains us.

Stories were told orally by tribe elders from generation to generation. With many advancements came new ways to tell stories, from written language to books, from paintings to photography, and photos to moving pictures: modern cinema.

There are many ways we enjoy movies. We can watch the latest releases at the movie theater or on streaming platforms.

Movies are everywhere! They are the work of many talented and creative people collaborating to create a finished film. From laborers, artists, and technicians to producers and directors...they all work together to bring a story to life.

Now, the process of creating a movie starts with the screenwriter. The screenwriter is responsible for creating a document that presents the exciting adventures the heroes will face in an explosive narrative made to entertain us. This document is what we call the movie script. That is what you'll learn to write with this book!

A *screenplay* or *script*, for short, is a document about 90 to 110 pages long that contains the story of the movie that a film crew will create. The script has all the elements needed to move it from the script's pages to the silver screen.

Now comes the question: What is a story? A story is a collection of events that, when told in a logical order, creates a narrative that entertains. As screenwriters, we call these events *plot points*. Plot points help move the story forward by bringing changes, conflicts, and challenges to the hero or the protagonist. Remember that a story can have multiple plot points, yet a certain number of plot points are necessary when writing a script.

The Greek philosopher Aristotle once identified three segments of a story: a beginning, a middle, and an end. This idea is accurate for most stories, even for a short joke you tell your best friend. For example:

Beginning: Two muffins were sitting in an oven.

Middle: One turned to the other and said, "Wow, it's pretty hot in here."

End: The other one shouted, "Wow, a talking muffin!"

In the late 1970s, screenwriter Syd Field applied Aristotle's concept of a beginning, a middle, and an end to what we now know as the three-act structure. This structure breaks down the script into three parts: Act One, Act Two, and Act Three.

Each act has its specific plot points that help the story move forward from (you guessed it) the beginning (act one) to the middle (act two) to the end (act three).

THE THREE-ACT STRUCTURE

As mentioned before, the three-act structure, also called the *paradigm structure*, was popularized by Syd Field in the late 1970s, and it is still used today by modern screenwriters. Syd Field broke the story down into three acts. Let's start with...

ACT ONE

The first act is always the setup of the story. It introduces the protagonist and the situation they will face. In a feature film, it is about twenty-five to thirty minutes long.

Act one contains two major plot points. The first plot point is the *inciting incident*. The inciting incident is the event that sets the story forward. For example, when Spider-Man (Tom Holland) interferes with Doctor Strange's (Benedict Cumberbatch) spells and cracks open the multi-verse in *Spider-Man: No Way Home* (2021). This event presents the problem that will affect Peter Parker for the rest of the story.

The inciting incident occurs early in the story, usually in the movie's first ten minutes. Remember that this is the hook to grab your audience's attention.

The second main plot point in Act One is the *key incident*. Also known as *plot point 1,* it occurs at or slightly before the end of the first act. In *Star Wars: Episode IV – A New Hope* (1977), the key incident happens when Luke Skywalker (Mark Hamill) returns to his home to find it destroyed by imperial stormtroopers. Luke decides to go with Obi-Wan Kenobi (Sir Alec Guinness) to take R2-D2 and C-3PO to the rebellion.

The key incident presents what the story is about and helps propel the protagonist on their journey. The protagonist is the main character of the story.

And there is the first act of your script: the beginning of the story, which leads us to...

ACT TWO

The second act is where you develop your story. It is usually from fifty to sixty pages long in a feature film. Many plot points change the story and propel it in a new direction. This act includes challenges and opposition to the protagonist.

Like the first act, act two has two main plot points. The first plot point is the *midpoint*. As the name suggests, this event happens in the middle of the script. It usually presents a low point for the protagonist. In *Star Wars: Episode IV – A New Hope,* this moment comes when the *Millennium Falcon* is captured by the Death Star's tractor beam when they arrive at the Alderaan System. And oh, boy, are our heroes in trouble!

The second plot point in Act Two is *plot point 2*. This event is the point of no return that leads our protagonist to the end of the story. This happens when Luke Skywalker volunteers to be an X-wing fighter pilot to fight at the Battle of Yavin. This event leads us to…

ACT THREE

The third act is the ending of the story. It is usually the same length as Act One: twenty-five to thirty minutes long. This act will lead us to a plot point called the *climax*. This is the point where our protagonist either wins or loses their challenge.

The final plot point is called the *resolution*. This presents our protagonist in their new world.

And that is the three-act structure. Remember that every story has a beginning, a middle, and an end that takes our heroes through their adventures.

THE LOGLINE

Now that we know a story has a beginning, a middle, and an end, we have to come up with ideas to transform into a new story. Ideas come in many ways. Maybe something that happened to you the other day. Perhaps it is a book you read at your library. Or a fantastic movie or a video game that gives you an idea to explore and develop.

One way to create an idea is through the *logline*. The logline is a short description of your concept, and can also be used to pitch your screenplay to people who want to help you produce your story.

A logline explains your story using twenty-five to thirty words or one to two sentences. Your logline presents the who, what, and why, which describes what your story is about.

For example:

> *A valiant teddy bear must lead a group of unlikely heroes to confront the Queen of Spiders before she corrupts an innocent girl's soul.*

If you'll notice, the name of the hero teddy bear isn't included because it is not necessary in the logline. All that is needed is to identify the protagonist with a noun and an adjective. For example, a scaredy-cat ghost catcher, a nervous doctor, a brave policeman, etc.

Here is a template you can use:

"When a/n (insert PROTAGONIST) (insert INCITING INCIDENT), s/he/they must first overcome a/n (insert ANTAGONIST) in order to (insert GOAL) by (insert HOW)."

> *When a naive farmer finds a message from a captured princess, he must overcome a powerful warlord in order to save the galaxy by destroying a deadly weapon.*

It is essential not to confuse a logline with a tagline. A tagline is a marketing blurb that appears on a movie poster or advertisement. Examples of taglines are, "In space, no one can hear you scream" or "If adventure has a name, it must be Indiana Jones."

EXERCISE 1

Using the logline template, create three loglines and then select your favorite logline. This logline will be the idea you use to develop a short film script.

ELEMENTS OF THE SCRIPT

Scriptwriting is very different from prose writing. When writing a novel or a short story, you can write freely, and the story can be as descriptive as you like. On the other hand, screenwriting is a whole different story (no pun intended).

In screenwriting, we use a specific format to create the movie script. The formatting rules are fundamental to remember since they're used as a standard in the movie industry.

The industry uses this specific format because one page of the script is more or less equal to one minute of film. This format helps in figuring out how long the movie will be. In theory, a ten-page script would be similar to a short film about ten minutes long. A ninety-page script would make a ninety-minute feature film.

This, too, is why we use short descriptions in a script. Using the correct formatting rules will make your script look like this:

```
1  EXT. SCENE HEADER OR SLUG LINE

   This part is the Action Paragraph or Description Paragraph.
   Here, you will present what the camera is viewing at the
   moment. You can have action, sound effects, character
   introductions, etc.

                        2 DIALOGUE CUE
                     3 (parenthetical)
                  4 This is the character's dialogue.
                     This is what the actor will speak
                     on cue.

                                         5 TRANSITION:


   INT. NEW SCENE

   More action or description is needed to continue the story.

                        DIALOGUE CUE
                  More dialogue goes here!

                                         FADE OUT.
```

1. Scene headers and action: left margin 1.5" and right margin 7.5"

2. Character cue: left margin 3.5"

3. Parenthetical: left margin 3"

4. Dialogue: left margin 2.5" to right margin 6"

5. Transition: left margin 6"

SCENE HEADERS (SLUGLINES)

Scene headers (also called *sluglines*) give a wide variety of information about the scene. They are always typed in caps.

They can be short:

```
BOB
```

Or they can be long and complicated:

```
EXT. BOB'S HOUSE - LAWN - CLOSE ON GARDEN TABLE -
EARLY MORNING (JUNE 15, 2022)
```

The slugline may contain up to five pieces of information, including:

1. Interior or exterior shot
2. Location
3. Type of shot
4. Subject of shot
5. Time of day

INTERIOR OR EXTERIOR

This indicates whether the scene occurs in an interior (INT.) or exterior (EXT.) location. For example:

```
INT. HOSPITAL
EXT. MOVIE THEATER
```

Sometimes, your character might be inside a car. In this case, the scene header would look like this:

```
EXT. AUSTIN FREEWAY/INT. AUDREY'S PORSCHE - DAY
```

or

EXT./INT. AUDREY'S PORSCHE - DAY

What if the action takes place in an open-air stadium? It is still an exterior location:

EXT. DODGERS STADIUM - NIGHT

Just think "INT." for indoors and "EXT." for outdoors.

LOCATION

Location shows where the scene takes place.

EXT. YAVIN IV - REBEL BASE
INT. F-14 JET FIGHTER - COCKPIT
INT. EL CONQUISTADOR HOTEL - PENTHOUSE
SUITE - BATHROOM
EXT. SHANE'S BACKYARD

A scene header may have more than one location element, but note that the elements go in order from general to specific, with each element separated by a hyphen:

EXT. PACIFIC OCEAN - USS ENTERPRISE -
FLIGHT DECK - LOADING PLATFORM - DAY

TYPE OF SHOTS

Sometimes, as a writer, you might want to suggest a specific type of shot. These may include establishing shots, wide shots, close shots, extreme close-ups, insert shots, etc. You don't need to have them in the script since the director selects the type of shot in the *production script* (see "production script" in the glossary). Regardless, it is still good to know this information.

A. CLOSE-UP

A close-up is a shot that focuses closely on a subject. The writer can indicate close-ups in different ways:

```
CLOSE - ANGELA'S EYES
CLOSE SHOT - ANGELA'S EYES
CLOSE-UP - ANGELA'S EYES
CLOSE ON ANGELA'S EYES
CLOSE ANGLE ON ANGELA'S EYES
```

B. WIDE SHOT

A wide shot moves away from the subject and includes the scenery.

```
WIDE - OLD SETTLER'S PARK
WIDE SHOT - OLD SETTLER'S PARK
WIDE ANGLE - OLD SETTLER'S PARK
WIDE ON OLD SETTLER'S PARK
WIDE ANGLE ON OLD SETTLER'S PARK
```

Notice that when the preposition "on" is used in the shot, a hyphen is not.

C. MEDIUM SHOT

Between the wide shot and the close-up is the medium shot. This shot shows the subject from the midsection up to the head.

```
MED. SHOT - EDDIE AND ALEX
```

SUBJECT OF THE SHOT

The writer uses the subject of the shot to focus attention on a specific subject or a group of subjects. It can be a subject as small as a mouse or as enormous as a mountain range:

```
BOB
ALEX AND EDDIE
HIMALAYAS
```

Subjects may include descriptors:

```
CRYING GIRL
```

Keep in mind that scene headers don't include action. Do not use:

```
SPIDER-MAN KICKS GREEN GOBLIN OFF GLIDER
SURGEON MAKES INCISION
```

Instead, write it like this:

```
SPIDER-MAN
kicks the Green Goblin off the glider.
SURGEON
makes the incision.
```

TIME OF DAY

This element shows the time of day the scene is taking place. Time of day is important because it helps the production team to plan for the shot. There are two basic options:

DAY: indicates daytime
NIGHT: indicates nighttime

For example:

```
EXT. NAKATOMI PLAZA - LOBBY ENTRANCE - NIGHT
INT. FRED'S BEDROOM - NIGHT
INT. GORDON'S OFFICE - DAY
```

There are various options for placing time information.

```
INT. DANNY'S CAR - MINUTES LATER
EXT. REBEL BASE - EVENING
INT. STARBUCKS - MORNING
```

DESCRIPTION

Description, or action, shows what is seen and heard on the screen. It includes introductions and descriptions of the characters, actions, sound effects, special effects, etc. The action shows us what is happening.

A description is written in the present tense:

```
Steve peeks over the door. His shield lies
on the floor, A MACHINE GUN LOADS, Steve
lunges for the shield, a machine gun FIRES
at him, and the BULLETS RICOCHET over the
wall.
```

Action paragraphs can have multiple lines on the page:

```
A cacophony of murmurs lifts the air of the
hall. Ushers lead evening-dressed people
to their seats. A Beautiful Lady holds her
program booklet excitedly. Her Date smiles
and nods at her. The lights dim. The murmurs
cease. The curtains open at the stage where
```

the stage lights slowly brighten and reveal
a simple yet regal room.

You can break this into smaller paragraphs:

A cacophony of murmurs lifts the air of the
hall. Ushers lead evening-dressed people
to their seats.

A Beautiful Lady holds her program booklet
excitedly. Her Date smiles and nods at her.

The lights dim. The murmurs cease.

The curtains open at…

THE STAGE

…where the stage lights slowly brighten
and reveal a simple yet regal room.

Here's how it looks on a script page:

```
INT. THEATER AUDITORIUM - NIGHT

A cacophony of murmurs lifts the air of the hall. Ushers lead
evening-dressed people to their seats.

A BEAUTIFUL LADY holds her program booklet excitedly. Her
DATE smiles and nods at her.

The lights dim. The murmurs cease.

The curtains open at...

THE STAGE

...where the stage lights slowly brighten, revealing a simple
yet regal room.

From stage left, THE ACTOR, a man in his mid-30s in royal
guise, stoically walks towards center stage.

The Actor, in character, scans the stage to ensure he is
alone in the room.

The Actor closes his eyes, takes a deep breath, and slowly
opens them.

                    THE ACTOR
          To be, or not to be, that is the
          question...

THE AUDIENCE

...looks on with undivided attention.

THE ACTOR

...ignores the audience and takes the stage by storm.

                    THE ACTOR (CONT'D)
          Whether 'tis nobler in the mind to
          suffer the slings and arrows of
          outrageous fortune, or to take arms
          against a sea of troubles, and by
          opposing end them? To die: to
          sleep; No more; and by a sleep to
          say we end the heart-ache and the
          thousand natural shocks that flesh
          is heir to, 'tis a consummation
          devoutly to be wish'd.

At the...
```

Breaking the description into smaller paragraphs makes the action easier to read and creates a tempo. It also makes the page look dynamic. Some writers tend to limit their paragraphs to four or five lines. I like to have a three-line limit.

CAPITALIZATION

Writers use caps in a description of action to indicate the following:

1. Introducing *new characters*
2. Indicating *sound effects*
3. Show a *camera shot*

```
The Lotus Elise drifts. TIRES SCREECH and
leave long marks on the road. MICHAEL
STEVENS grips the steering wheel and spins
it. CAMERA CLOSE ON his face as he grins.
```

You should only use caps when a speaking character appears for the first time in the script. You don't need to use caps with nonspeaking characters, but it's okay if you do.

```
BRUCE WAYNE stares at the giant computer
screen. A computer file opens, and a video
of a man with a shotgun plays.
Bruce grabs a coffee mug and drinks.
```

Sound effects are only capitalized in the script if the effects are not done naturally by the actor. Things like gunshots, car crashes, lightning, crying babies, horns honking, spaceships flying, etc., can be in caps.

You shouldn't capitalize things like the following: on-screen actors laughing, crying, coughing, sneezing, clapping, snapping their fingers, singing, etc.

```
Mary grabs the bottle of scotch. Her
hands tremble as she removes the cap. She
tosses the BOTTLE against the wall, and
it SHATTERS. Mary drops to her knees and
cries.
```

Camera shots are also capitalized. Keep in mind that you don't capitalize "camera" when it is an actual prop.

```
The Ballerina dances directly AT CAMERA.
The Photographer points his camera at her.
```

DIALOGUE

Dialogue consists of three elements:

1. Name of the character speaking (cue).
2. The words that the actor speaks.
3. Any parenthetical direction specifying how the line is spoken.

```
              CHARACTER CUE
             (parenthetical)
        This is the spoken line.
```

CHARACTER

The character's name must be consistent in the script. A *character cue* is a place where a character's name appears in the script. If the name in the character cue is "MICHAEL," then don't change it to "CAPTAIN MICHAEL," "MICKEY," or any other name. This could confuse the reader (and the casting director) into thinking they are multiple characters.

V.O. AND O.S.

V.O. stands for *voice-over*. It is used by the writer when a character is speaking off the screen and at a different physical location. The character could be a narrator, someone calling from a phone, a radio deejay, etc.

```
Michael presses the play button on the
answering machine.
```

> BOB (V.O.)
> Michael? Michael! Pick
> up the phone! Pete's got
> his finger stuck in the
> PlayStation again!

O.S. stands for *off-screen*. It is used when the character that speaks is out of the frame of the screen, but they are at the exact physical location:

```
Ted turns at the sound of Bob's calls from
outside the garage door.
```

> BOB (O.S.)
> (sings in high pitch)
> Teddy is a loser. Teddy
> cries like a bay-bee! Boo-
> hoo! Bay-bee! Woo-hoo!

PARENTHETICAL

A *parenthetical* is a set of instructions that can appear in the dialogue to indicate how to deliver the line to the actor. Parentheticals can be easily overused or misused by a writer. Many actors and directors tend to ignore them. Still, it can be used by the writer as a very effective tool if used wisely.

> MICHELLE
> (whispers)
> Juanita... Juanita! Get in
> here!

Or...

Gregor and Mikael argue in Russian. John
sighs and stands.

                    JOHN
               (at Gregor)
          You shut up!
               (at Mikael)
          You keep talking.

TRANSITIONS

Transitions are the various methods to change from one scene to
the next. They can include *cuts, dissolves, fades,* and *wipes.*

FADES

A *fade-in* is a gradual transition from black to a photographed
image. A *fade-out* is the complete opposite: it transitions from image
to black. "FADE IN" is typed on the left margin of the page, and a
colon follows it:

FADE IN:

On the other hand, a fade-out is set six inches from the left edge
of the page, and it is always followed by a period.

                                        FADE OUT.

Except for "FADE IN," all transitions are typed six inches from
the left edge of the page.

Traditionally, feature and short film scripts use "FADE IN" at the
beginning of the script and "FADE OUT" at the end. Remember that

they are unnecessary since it is assumed that the film fades in at the beginning and out at the end.

"FADE IN" and "FADE OUT" can also be used by writers in TV scripts to indicate an act (and commercial) break.

You can also use "FADE TO BLACK" or "FADE TO WHITE" as an alternative to "FADE OUT":

```
                    FADE TO BLACK.


                    FADE TO WHITE.
```

CUTS

"CUT" is the most common transition in screenwriting. It presents an instantaneous shift from one shot to the next. It appears six inches from the left edge of the page, and a colon follows it:

```
                              CUT TO:
```

An entire script can be written without this transition since it is always assumed that there is a cut from one scene to the next.

There are some variations of the "CUT TO" transition. You can use "HARD CUT TO" for jarring transitions; "MATCH CUT TO" if the first shot matches the second shot visually or thematically; or "CUT TO BLACK," where, for dramatic effect, the image cuts to a black screen.

DISSOLVES

A *dissolve* is a gradual transition between images. It is used to denote the passage of time:

```
The Spider Queen leads Emily inside
the closet, and they disappear. Rickles
struggles but passes out.
```

```
                                    DISSOLVE TO:

INT. EMILY'S ROOM - MINUTES LATER

Hans shakes Rickles.

                    HANS
          Wake up!
```

Just like cuts, there are many variations of the dissolve. One of them is the ripple dissolve, in which a ripple effect of the image is used to show a transition to a dream or imaginary sequence.

WIPES

A *wipe* is a stylized transition in which a new image slides, or wipes, on top of the old one:

```
OPTIMUS PRIME

transforms  into  a  truck  and  drives
away.

                              WIPE TO:

EXT. THE ARK - DAY

Optimus  Prime's  (TRUCK  MODE)  TIRES
SCREECH,  and  he  skids  to  stop.
```

TITLE PAGE

The *title page* is significant since it contains the script's title, the writer's name, and the writer's contact information. Like the script itself, it is written in size twelve Courier font. The title is written in the center and four inches down from the top of the page. The title is also underlined without quotation marks:

THE SHOW MUST GO ON

After the title comes "Written by," followed by the writer's name. This information is centered on the page and appears four lines below the title:

COOL ADVENTURE

Written by

Young Screenwriter

On the lower left corner of the title page comes the contact information, including address, phone, and email:

    123 My Address St.
    City, State Zip Code
    (123) 555-4567
    myemail@email.com

The contact information is typed one inch from the left edge of the page.

COOL ADVENTURE

Written by

Young Screenwriter

123 My Address St.
City, State Zip Code
(123) 555-4567
myemail@email.com

ADVANCED TECHNIQUES

The following are not elements per se but techniques that can help when writing certain scenes in the script.

INSERT SHOT

An *insert shot* is a special close-up that changes any object into the main subject of the shot to show a detail. For example:

```
Maggie  wakes  up  next  to  Emily.  Maggie
kisses her daughter and looks at the table.

INSERT - CLOCK

The bright red LED display: "11:38 AM"

                              BACK TO SCENE

                    MAGGIE
        Ugh.
```

FLASHBACK AND DREAM SEQUENCE

A *flashback* is an event that occurred in the past relative to the current scene or event. On the other hand, a dream sequence is a dream a character has at the moment. These are two very different events but are very similar in terms of formatting.

In a flashback, the word "FLASHBACK" appears underlined, followed by a hyphen in the scene header:

```
FLASHBACK - EXT. SCHOOL - DAY
```

This is the same in a dream sequence:

DREAM SEQUENCE - EXT. SCHOOL - DAY

You then write the action, description, and dialogue as usual. When you end the flashback or the dream sequence, you can indicate it in the following way:

END FLASHBACK.

END DREAM SEQUENCE.

These indications work as transitions to the next scene. Let's look at the following example:

DREAM SEQUENCE - EXT. AVALON - DAY

Alba opens her eyes in a daze. After a second, she finds herself in a saddle atop the back of a Green Dragon.

                    DRAGON
                  (laughs)
            Awake? Good!
                  (yells)
            Let us fly!

The Dragon beats his mighty wings and takes flight. Alba holds on to the saddle.

                    ALBA
            Whoa!

                    END DREAM SEQUENCE.

MONTAGE

A *montage* is a group of images, often accompanied by music, showing the passage of time. This technique presents a series of events, like a get-together or a date.

```
ARCADE - MONTAGE

Eddie and Alba play Street Fighter. Eddie
smashes the buttons to attack. Alba expertly
counters and knocks Eddie's character out.

They play a virtual reality game. Eddie
fires his gun in short, controlled bursts.
Alba fires wildly and screams.

They play Whac-A-Mole side by side. Prize
tickets burst from the machine.

Eddie exchanges the tickets for a teddy
bear at the counter. Alba smiles as she
hugs the bear.
```

If you noticed, each paragraph functions as an individual event or shot.

POV

A *POV*, or *point of view*, is a type of shot that presents what a specific character sees at that moment. You can start a POV shot similarly to a scene header and end it with a "BACK TO SCENE" blurb. For example:

```
EXT. PARK - NIGHT

Emily hastily walks across the dark path.
Something BRUSHES against a nearby bush.
Emily stops in her tracks.

EMILY'S POV

A tiny black kitten walks from under the
bush and MEOWS.

BACK TO SCENE

Emily breathes in relief. She kneels in
front of the kitten.

                    EMILY
          Here, kitty, kitty, kitty!
```

EXERCISE 2

Now that you have the basic knowledge of script formatting, you can start writing your script...as long as you already have a story. In exercise A, you created three story ideas via a logline. Your next step is to develop a *treatment*. The treatment is simply a document written in a prose format.

In the treatment, you'll write your story with a beginning, a middle, and an end.

Treatments may contain many pages. Some may be ten pages or more. This document can be one to two pages long for a short film script. For a feature film script, it is generally ten pages or more.

Here is a template you can use:

[TITLE] by [AUTHOR]

LOGLINE

Logline goes here.

ACT ONE

Act one goes here.

ACT TWO

Act two goes here.

ACT THREE

Act three goes here.

Cool Adventure by Young Screenwriter

LOGLINE

When a cowardly lion escapes from the zoo, he must overcome an obsessive zoo keeper in order to find his freedom by reaching a cruise to Africa.

ACT ONE

Lorem ipsum dolor sit amet, consectetur adipiscing elit. Proin dui urna, sodales id elementum ut, mollis nec sapien. Proin erat nisl, molestie eget ipsum id, volutpat auctor sem. Phasellus ornare at arcu at convallis. Donec placerat pharetra dolor nec rutrum. Cras orci leo, viverra sed justo nec, molestie bibendum nibh. Pellentesque odio turpis, rutrum id sapien id, lobortis placerat lorem. Vestibulum eu odio consequat elit auctor suscipit. Cras non justo maximus, accumsan nibh sed, pellentesque diam. Duis egestas elementum pharetra. Integer a consequat turpis, sed rutrum urna. Phasellus convallis, nulla eget tempus fermentum, lacus tellus congue massa, nec posuere lectus nisi in felis. Nunc maximus ac turpis vitae eleifend. Aliquam posuere libero sit amet turpis facilisis, et luctus arcu pulvinar.

ACT TWO

Aliquam erat volutpat. Class aptent taciti sociosqu ad litora torquent per conubia nostra, per inceptos himenaeos. Ut ut venenatis purus. Sed at ligula sed mi sagittis venenatis ultrices at nibh. Praesent pharetra pulvinar risus, eu sodales nisl interdum et. Nulla semper enim quis fermentum iaculis. Praesent tincidunt neque id neque hendrerit porta. Nulla quis libero finibus, semper ex in, dictum massa. Mauris fringilla dictum fermentum. Suspendisse et neque ac turpis efficitur molestie in eu felis. Ut non nunc id ligula convallis rutrum quis nec metus. Cras hendrerit rhoncus tortor ac rhoncus. Suspendisse pulvinar, tortor quis mattis maximus, ligula eros aliquam quam, eu porttitor mauris nulla a nulla. Donec tincidunt metus sit amet nulla luctus dignissim. Donec euismod, velit ultricies mollis pulvinar, justo lacus efficitur sapien, eget tempor lorem risus ac dui. Donec posuere odio sed metus sollicitudin sollicitudin.

ACT THREE

Nam sed est ultricies, pretium mi nec, laoreet nisi. Praesent sit amet lectus ac quam molestie accumsan. Aenean interdum sodales ex, sit amet pellentesque lectus fermentum quis. Quisque lacinia neque a nisl pretium, eget tempus velit interdum. Fusce varius dictum turpis vel dapibus. Etiam ornare pharetra ante, ac dictum dui suscipit et. Quisque blandit nibh nisi, et ultricies magna pretium eu. Maecenas congue finibus tincidunt. Aliquam diam eros, vehicula id finibus vitae, pellentesque at erat. Maecenas laoreet id sem quis maximus. Nam vel mi erat. Vivamus fermentum eleifend neque, sed porttitor lectus rhoncus vel. Sed tempor vulputate elementum. Duis sit amet neque ut orci eleifend aliquet. Donec lacinia risus eu nunc sollicitudin consequat. Nullam facilisis nisl vitae odio volutpat aliquam.

Using this template, you will select one of your loglines and write your story treatment. This activity will guide you toward the development of your script!

CHARACTER AND DIALOGUE

As important as it is to have a compelling story, the story should be anchored by having inspiring heroes, insidious villains, helpful allies, challenging henchmen, and other characters who bring your story to life. Characters are crucial to a story. With characters, you can have action, conflict, drama, and humor that entertain viewers and readers alike. Without characters, your story will not move forward to its conclusion.

Most characters' tales follow the archetypes of the hero's journey or monomyth. This theory was created by writer and scholar Joseph Campbell. It examines the hero's steps during their adventure when facing obstacles and their triumphant return to the ordinary world.

Campbell postulated that different myths from different civilizations follow the same steps or journey of the hero. As a result, the hero's journey has influenced many writers and filmmakers, including George Lucas, James Cameron, and the Wachowski Sisters, among others.

Along with the steps of the hero's journey, Campbell also postulates that the characters of these myths and stories follow a group of universal archetypes of characters who populate these stories.

Let us explore those archetypes:

1. The Hero: The hero is the character with whom the audience identifies. They must overcome their flaws in order to grow in wisdom and maturity.

2. The Mentor: The mentor is the hero's guiding figure. They provide teachings and gifts that may serve as weapons for the hero along their journey. The mentor acts as the hero's conscience, like the veteran giving advice to the rookie.

3. The Herald: The herald issues a challenge to the hero and provides the call to adventure. A herald can be a character or an object that brings a message.

4. The Threshold Guardian: The threshold guardian provides obstacles for the hero to overcome. These characters tend to be henchmen or lieutenants of the main villain (see number 8, the shadow). They test the hero on his way to face the villain. Defeating the threshold guardians provides growth to the hero.

5. The Ally: Sometimes, the hero can't continue his journey alone. He may need a companion who will share the hero's burden. An ally may start antagonistic toward the hero. Still, the ally's outlook usually changes once they gain respect and admiration (see number 6, the shapeshifter) for the hero once the hero earns their respect.

6. The Shapeshifter: A shapeshifter is a character who constantly changes from the hero's point of view. The shapeshifter can often be an ally of the hero, like a fellow cop in a buddy film.

7. The Trickster: The trickster(s) add humor and fun to the adventure. They give the audience a much-needed break when times get gloomy or tense.

8. The Shadow: The shadow is the villain in your story and creates a threat or conflict for the hero. The shadow can mirror the hero in some ways. The shadow might also be what the hero becomes if they succumb to the temptations of evil; thus, the shadow highlights the hero's internal struggle.

The eight character archetypes of the hero's journey appear in many stories, myths, and movies. Now that we've identified the character archetypes, let's explore what makes a compelling character.

CHARACTER FLAWS

Characters have many traits that enable them to connect with the audience. The protagonist can be brave, hopeful, kind, and forgiving, but some traits can make a stronger bond between the character and the viewer. These are *character flaws*. Exciting characters have flaws to overcome, and these flaws bring growth to the character.

A flaw can obstruct the protagonist's journey to reach their goal. This flaw can be something like alcoholism, substance abuse, mental illness, sickness, etc. Other flaws can be character traits like vanity, hubris, mistrust, greed, narcissism, etc.

These flaws provide the hero with an opportunity to transform, thus moving your story forward. In order to have a story about transformation, the need for that change must be established by the writer. In *Who Framed Roger Rabbit?* Eddie Valiant turns to alcohol to try to ease the pain of the loss of his brother. Eddie must overcome his dependence on alcohol to save Toontown. Eddie grows as a character in overcoming this flaw, and the audience loves it!

Because the flaw reveals an aspect that can destroy the hero's opportunity for growth, it's presented as an opposite of the value of the story's theme (see Chapter 5). A flaw is a potential conflict for the protagonist and can cause problems for the hero, their friends, allies, and relationships.

Remember, too, that perfection doesn't exist in real life. If you describe your character as perfect, the audience will not find them relatable.

CONFLICT

Characters are defined by the challenges they face in their story. There is always a conflict that the character will face in hopes that they can overcome it. There are four types of conflict a protagonist might face:

1. Man against Man: This conflict happens when two characters are pitted against each other. This external conflict can be a

direct opposition or something more subtle: a conflict of desire (as in romance) or a family epic.

2. Man against Society: This conflict happens when characters make a moral choice against a man-made institution (such as the government) or are frustrated by social rules in meeting their goals.

3. Man against Nature: This conflict happens when the protagonist attempts to survive against the forces of nature.

4. Man against Self: This conflict is an internal struggle in which characters must overcome their nature or face two paths: good and evil or logic and emotion. This conflict is an excellent example of a character overcoming a flaw.

DIALOGUE

What is dialogue? It is a conversation between two or more people, presented as a part of a movie. You will find that conversations tend to be chaotic and disjointed. Next time you're in a public place, notice how people talk to each other. You can hear lots of "um" and "ah" or "uh." People tend to talk over each other to deliver an understandable message. Yet, movie dialogue is the exact opposite.

Dialogue is clear and concise. Dialogue is a means to push the story forward. Dialogue that doesn't move the story forward becomes boring; that's when you risk losing your audience.

Movie dialogue is not a real-life conversation. Real-life conversation is dull, trite, and disjointed. Movie dialogue creates conflict yet is subtle and uses *subtext* to give the lines more depth. Subtext is the meaning not stated by the character but lies beneath the surface.

Writing dialogue is not intended to capture reality. "Realistic dialogue" only gives a flavor of reality. It may sound real, but it is a deception. Dialogue follows a rhythm. It is clear and easily spoken.

Movie dialogue is compressed and moves rapidly. It moves back and forth between the characters, shifting power from one side to the other. Think of it as a tennis match. One player serves, and the other counters until one player misses the ball.

Keep subtext in mind. Subtext is a message that is not spoken but inferred. After all, characters rarely say what they mean.

EXERCISE 3

Congratulations! By now, you should have a completed story treatment. You should have all the events and characters to make up your short film script!

This exercise is broken into two parts. The first part will help you develop your characters. Please take a few minutes to get to know your characters by writing a small biography of them: what they like, what they don't like, and what flaw(s) they must overcome. In addition to their biography, write a page or two describing how your characters do their laundry. Does anything interesting happen? How do they face the ordeal?

You can continue with your story once you get to know your characters better. The next step in the process is to organize yourself. An outline will help break down your treatment into smaller parts to help you write your short film script better.

Use the following template to create your outline:

[TITLE]

ACT ONE

    1) First image
    2) Inciting incident
    3) Key incident

ACT TWO

    4) First attempt to solve the problem
    5) Increase the severity of the problem
    6) Lowest point for the character
    7) Plot point 2: point of no return

ACT THREE

    8) Tension at full peak
    9) Climax
    10) Resolution

PACING, ACTION, SEQUENCE, AND GENRE

PACING

Every story has a rhythm. This rhythm helps create a beat and maintain tempo. It helps to keep your story exciting, even in slower scenes. Some scenes can be slower; some can be faster. Remember that if you place too many details in your script, you will slow down the pace.

Pace your script according to the action on the screen. A dramatic moment can be slower yet engaging. A car chase will be faster and more exciting!

Many choreographed action scenes are scant reads on the page. They show the overall action but don't go over every detail to avoid slowing the reading experience. Slower scenes, which convey the mood of the setting, or tender character moments can be more descriptive. You want the audience to slow down and bond with your characters. Even if you're writing a slower scene, try to enter the scene late and leave the scene early. If you ignore this, you risk having the character do something like pulling into the driveway and opening the door, wasting valuable story time in unnecessary details. This will also happen if you leave the scene too late. For example:

```
EXT. LONESOME VALLEY - DAY
```

A group of bandits desperately ride their horses. GUNSHOTS ring high. Horses NEIGH. The OUTLAW, a man in his early 40s with a duster and wide-brim hat, leads the group.

The bandits follow the Outlaw. Their horses carry sacks of money on their sides.

GOLDEN TOOTH, in his late 30s, dearly holds his bag.

GRIZZLY, a big man with a beard in his 30s, wildly fires behind him.

Next to him rides THE KID, in his late teens, with panic in his eyes.

Far behind them ride a posse of ten men led by the SHERIFF, a man in gray clothes, chevron style mustache, and a badge on his chest.

Next to him rides the DEPUTY, a handsome man with a square jaw in his early 20s. The other men ride along. They FIRE their guns.

As you can see, the scene starts at a high dramatic point, thus avoiding unnecessary filler. Short introductions and descriptions of the characters follow this. In the end, we don't linger on the scene. We leave early in the action to the next scene.

TIPS FOR SCENE PACING

1. As advised, get to the objective of the scene quickly and then cut out of the scene as soon as possible.

2. Examine the objective of the scene and use this as a guidepost for pacing.

3. Every scene in your screenplay must provide insight and information about your character's decisions, motivations, obstacles, and goals.

4. Each scene must have a strong arc (see "arc" in glossary), a clear objective, and an event or action that propels the story forward.

5. The scene must have a purpose. If the scene lacks a purpose, then it will likely be cut out and end up in the deleted scenes section on the Blu-ray or DVD.

ACTION

Every film has action. No matter what genre your story is, the story is not static on the screen. And now that you understand that film is action, there is a little something we call the *action scene*. The action scene is a moment that creates excitement, conflict, strife, and entertainment!

Action is *exciting*! Hard-core heroes and femmes fatales fight, drive, jump, kick, shoot to kill, kick butt, and chew bubble gum...and they are always out of bubble gum.

Action writing should keep your reader at the edge of the seat. It should be short and fast. Remember to write in the present tense with an active voice.

```
EXT. VILLAGE ENTRANCE - NIGHT

Hans dives to his side and avoids the
attack. Hans counterstrikes against the
Spider Queen, but she blocks each blow.

They engage in a deadly dance. Steel
CLASHES and RINGS.
```

Three Arachnids break rank and charge Hans.

Hans turns and strikes the first Arachnid. The Spider Queen thrusts with her swords, but Hans blocks the attack with ease.

The second Arachnid attempts to pounce on Hans. He evades, jumps on top of the Arachnid, and drives a sword through its back.

The third Arachnid passes by the Spider Queen. She impales the Arachnid Warrior. It explodes in a cloud of dust.

> SPIDER QUEEN
> (at Arachnids)
> Break rank again and die!
> Hans is mine and mine alone.

Hans grins.

> HANS
> Thank you!

WRITING ACTION

1. When writing action, you can use scene headers to break things up on the page.
2. It is not necessary to include very many details. Fight choreographers and stunt directors will plan those details.
3. Writing your paragraph with a maximum of three lines helps create a rhythm.
4. When writing dialogue in action, keep it short. "He's there!" "What the—" "Get her!" etc.

SEQUENCE

In filmmaking, a *sequence* is a group of scenes that form a cohesive narrative. The scheme of a sequence is represented in the following order:

Shot < Scene < Sequence

An example of a sequence is when Doctor Octopus (Alfred Molina) confronts Spider-Man (Tom Holland) at the bridge in *Spider-Man: No Way Home* (2021). Besides being a thrilling action sequence, it moves the story forward by showing the consequences of Peter Parker's meddling with the multi-verse.

A sequence, as well as the scene, must have a beginning, a middle, and an end. This is an individual story in the grand scheme of the story. This can have beats and rhythm to create tension and excitement. A well-paced dramatic sequence can be exciting—even if no punches are thrown.

A sequence has an end, which leads to the following sequence. It helps propel the story forward.

GENRE

Film genre is a way to categorize different styles of stories. Genres may change over time, but they help to identify what kind of story is presented and what type of audience the story is geared to.

Many genres can have multiple sub-genres or may combine two different genres: horror-comedy or drama-musical, for instance.

1. Action: Action films are exciting extravaganzas filled with fights, car chases, stunts, and nonstop motion designed for pure escapism.
2. Adventure: Often paired with action films, the adventure genre presents exciting stories filled with exotic locations and quests with death-defying danger and perils.

3. Comedy: Comedies are amusing yarns that use jokes, one-liners, and exaggerated characters or situations as part of the narrative.

4. Animation: Not a genre per se, but a medium that uses animated drawings to present a story. These can be shown in different genres, but, more often than not, they are paired with stories for families and children.

5. Drama: Dramas are serious, plot-driven stories with realistic characters and thought-provoking narratives.

6. Epics/Historical: More of a sub-genre of drama films, this category includes costume dramas, historical dramas, and films that involve extravagant settings and costumes.

7. Horror: Horror films invoke our fears of the unknown and entertain us as much as they scare us.

8. Musicals: The hills are alive with the sound of music! Musicals use scores or songs as part of the narrative.

9. Sci-Fi: Visionary movies with a semi-scientific base. Sci-fi films are filled with mighty heroes, aliens, distant planets, futuristic technologies, and monsters.

10. War: War films present the horror of war; combat serves as the primary plot or background of the story.

11. Westerns: One of the oldest genres, these films depict moral stories set in the Old West and include recognizable character archetypes, plots, and situations.

EXERCISE 4

First, you came up with your script idea with the logline. After that, you developed your story with the treatment. Then you organized your story with the outline.

With those exercises and the topics you have read in this book, you are ready to write your first short film script!

You now possess all the tools to write a five- to ten-page script. If your story requires a few more pages, then go for it. Good luck, young screenwriter!

WRITING AND REWRITING

By now, you should have completed the first draft of your short film script. Great job! For some of you, the screenwriting experience may have been smooth. For others, this may have been a bit stressful. This is normal. Don't feel discouraged if you're having problems writing; this is called...

WRITER'S BLOCK

Writer's block is when a writer cannot place a single word on paper. When writer's block happens, the first thing to do is not panic. I mean it. Don't panic. It happens to the best of us. It happens to all of us. We find ourselves unable to place a single word on the page.

Causes of writer's block:

1. Timing: There may be a better time to work on your script, and the idea needs further development.
2. Fear: Many writers fear putting their ideas (and themselves) out in public for everyone to see and critique.
3. Perfectionism: The writer believes that the story must be perfect when the first word appears on the page. This causes the writer to wait for the "perfect" moment that will never come.

How to beat writer's block:

1. Go for a walk. Eliminate distractions. Sip some coffee. Listen to music. Change your environment. Play with LEGOs.
2. Some say that having tea and cookies can help!
3. Don't stress! Rest your brain a bit and be recharged.

REWRITE

After finishing your first draft, taking a break for a few days is recommended. This will rest your mind and make it easier to identify problems in your script; this is an integral part of the rewrite process. Rewrite is an instance of writing something again to alter or improve it. There is a saying in our trade that "writing is rewriting."

The benefits of rewriting are many. This process helps to identify not only typos or grammar issues but it helps to find problems with structure, character development, and dialogue. Rewriting is a natural part of the writing process. It is an expected step in the life of your script.

It is expected that a first draft will be a flawed product. Rarely, a first draft is a quality product. Remember that the quality of your first draft is not a measure of your quality as a writer.

During the rewrite process, identify whether your scene lacks conflict. If the scene doesn't have conflict or doesn't move your story forward, then remove it.

Identify plot holes and remove them. Does your character's actions move your story to the next plot point? Is there a purpose to the conflict in your scene? Do you have too many characters, and thus, you're unsure who your protagonist is?

Does your scene begin when the conflict starts, and does it end when the conflict ends? Remember to start late and get out early.

Check your dialogue. Does it reveal character? Does it revolve around the conflict of the scene? Does it have subtext and hidden meaning? If not, then remove or rewrite it. Are you using passive or active voice? Are your sentences saying what they need to communicate with the least words needed? The fewer words used, the more space you have for your story. Write economically!

TIGHTENING YOUR SCRIPT: DIALOGUE

1. When writing (initially) or rewriting, one of the first things you can do is to tighten your dialogue.
2. Be careful not to make your dialogue sound as it does in real life. Dialogue is *not* real-life conversation. You create the illusion of real life, but great dialogue gets larger than life and full of hidden meanings.
3. Remove small talk. Small talk can become filler, and filler never moves the story forward.

TIGHTENING YOUR SCRIPT: ACTION

1. One of the biggest mistakes a beginner writer will make is overwrite. Overwriting occurs when you use more words than you need in telling your story.
2. Keep your scene simple. Only write what is needed to understand the situation.
3. Cut-out action that doesn't move the story forward.
4. Watch out for overly detailed descriptions. Take time to read your script and trim the fat. Not only will you reduce your page count, but you'll have a faster-paced script as well.

TIGHTENING YOUR SCRIPT: FORMAT

1. Keep in mind that tightening your format is not cutting corners. *Do not* change the margins, font size, spacing, etc. Cheating in your formatting will be noticed.
2. Remember to use the three-line-per-paragraph format. It breaks the action and creates a faster-to-read page.

TONE AND THEME

Tone is the feeling a writer conveys with the written word and can be formal, somber, funny, serious, scary, etc. Tone can be set with dialogue, action, and the imagery in the script. Tone can also help us underscore our script's genre and make the genre clear to the audience. Tone sets the feeling of your story. If your story is a serious drama, don't write with a cheery voice. This will clash with your tone, and your reader will have the wrong emotional response.

Now, *theme* is the broad idea or message conveyed by the story. The theme is usually about life or human nature. Theme is the moral lesson the writer may imply indirectly using a subtle approach. For example, *Star Wars: A New Hope* (1977) presents various themes during its narrative, including good vs. evil, hope and spirituality vs. technology, maturity, and a warning of the dangers of hubris. The script's tone is heavy in swashbuckling action and set with humor from the antics of R2-D2 and C-3PO.

EXERCISE 5

At this point, you may show your script to someone you trust (such as a friend or teacher) and listen to the feedback they provide. Then, based on the notes received and the information of this chapter, you are ready to rewrite your script.

WHAT'S NEXT?

By now, you should have the second draft of your script. Excellent work! This is not the end, though. Revise your script with as many drafts as needed until you have the best script possible. This marks the point at which your script is ready to be produced.

Before you show your script to a potential producer, ensure you protect your work by registering it. There are two types of script registration. There is the WGA registration and the U.S. copyright registration.

WHAT IS THE WGA?

The WGA is the Writers Guild of America. It is a labor union representing writers working in film, radio, TV, and related industries. The WGA protects the rights of writers, including matters regarding pay and labor disputes. They also offer services and benefits like a credit union, health benefits, retirement packages, etc.

WHAT IS COPYRIGHT?

Copyright is a legal right that provides the creator of a piece of intellectual property exclusive rights on how the work is used and distributed. These rights vary from country to country and run for a limited time, including the writer's lifetime and up to seventy years after the writer's demise. After that period, the work becomes part of the public domain.

REGISTRATION WITH THE WGA

1. Registration with the WGA only creates a public record of a claim to ownership.
2. If you have a legal dispute, the WGA can send a representative to testify with proof of registration date.
3. Registration lasts five years. At this point, it can be extended to five more years.
4. This registration *is not* a replacement for an actual copyright.

REGISTRATION FOR COPYRIGHT

1. Copyright provides proof of ownership of your work.
2. Copyright does not protect an idea. It protects how that idea is expressed.
3. Registration is required before a lawsuit can be brought to court.

CHOOSING BETWEEN REGISTRATION AND COPYRIGHT

Remember that the WGA registration does not substitute for the copyright registration. The WGA only provides proof of registration. The U.S. copyright provides proof of ownership.

You may utilize both the U.S. copyright and the WGA for better protection. If you only use one, use the U.S. copyright.

WEBSITES

U.S. Copyright Office: http://www.copyright.gov
WGA West: http://www.wga.org

WHAT'S NEXT?

After revising your script (to the best possible draft), register it. You will have a few options on what to do next.

SHOOT IT

- There are many options for screenwriters who want to produce their short films. First, get feedback from people you trust. This feedback will help you improve your script.
- Be social. Social media can be a positive tool if used correctly. If you crowdfund your project, having a solid social presence can help convince people to fund your project.
- If you are producing your script yourself, rewrite it to fit within the budget you manage to attain. Why waste thousands of dollars on an explosion if a simple punch in the face will work?
- If possible, shoot in locations you can access easily: a friend's house, a local business a friend owns, etc.
- If you want a full-length feature produced, making a short film based on one of the most exciting scenes can help generate interest in the original full-length feature script.
- Lastly, don't be afraid to adapt your feature script to other media forms (graphic novels, TV, video games, etc.). This may help get your initial idea out there and into your desired format somewhere down the line.

FILM FESTIVALS AND COMPETITIONS

Submitting your script to a competition can be a rewarding experience. If selected, you connect with peers and people who work in the industry, creating valuable contacts. Even placing as a quarterfinalist looks good on your writing resume.

COMPETITIONS

1. Academy Nicholl Fellowships (www.oscars.org/nicholl): Presented by the Academy of Motion Pictures Arts and Sciences.
2. Austin Film Festival (www.austinfilmfestival.com): This festival includes conferences, presentations of new movies, screenwriting and teleplay competitions, seminars, a pitch fest, etc.
3. Final Draft Big Break (www.finaldraft.com/big-break-screen writing-contest/): Another major online competition sponsored by Final Draft.
4. Page International Awards (www.pageawards.com): One of the biggest screenplay competitions with multiple categories and genres.

CONTEST SUBMISSION PLATFORMS

1. FilmFreeway (www.filmfreeway.com): FilmFreeway makes it easy to discover and submit to hundreds of film festivals and screenplay contests worldwide.
2. Coverfly (www.coverfly.com): Much like FilmFreeway, Coverfly lets you upload your project to submit to many festivals and competitions. This service also tracks your performance as a writer in an easy-to-use platform.

CONCLUSION

By now, you have the basic knowledge of how to write a screenplay—well done! The best thing to do is to keep writing. The more you write, the more you master script formatting and the three-act structure. Also, watch as many movies and read as many movie scripts as possible.

And keep learning! Remember, this book provides basic information on screenwriting. You can find a ton of information and many great tutorials available online.

Plenty of great books show more techniques and advanced methods for writing movie scripts, such as *Screenplay* by Syd Field, *The Writer's Journey* by Christopher Vogler, and *The Hollywood Standard* by Christopher Riley.

Some many great schools and institutions offer creative writing and screenwriting courses and degrees.

The resources are there for you to learn and advance as a movie writer. So go on, young screenwriter, and write the future movies that will entertain us!

GLOSSARY

action scene. Exciting scene with fights, car chases, and stunts.

arc. Also known as a *story arc*. It is a progression of events represented by five components: exposition, rising action, climax, falling action, and resolution.

archetypes. A typical example of a person or thing.

climax. It is the most intense point and culmination of a story.

conflict. A fight or struggle between two parties.

copyright. The exclusive right to use and distribute intellectual property. This lasts until the creator's demise and up to seventy years later.

description. In screenwriting, it shows what is seen and heard on the actual screen. It includes introductions and descriptions of the characters, actions, sound effects, special effects, etc. The action shows us what is happening.

dialogue. This is what people are supposed to say according to the script.

dissolve. A transition where one image fades out and another image fades in. This denotes the passage of time.

dream sequence. A scene that presents a dream the character has.

flashback. A scene that shows an event that has happened in the past.

genre. It is a way to categorize the story type. It helps in defining who your audience is.

inciting incident. An event about ten minutes into a feature film. This event presents a problem that will affect the protagonist.

key incident. An event that presents what the story is about and propels the protagonist to their journey. Also known as plot point 1. This event happens at the end of Act One.

logline. A blurb that presents or explains your story idea in thirty-five words or less. It can also be used for pitching your idea to a producer.

midpoint. An event that happens in the middle of the script. This could show the lowest point for your protagonist or a small victory that doesn't resolve the main problem.

monomyth. Also known as the hero's journey. A theory created by Joseph Campbell stipulates that most stories across civilizations and geographical locations share the same events or plot points and the same character archetypes.

montage. A series of scenes that denotes the passage of time, usually presented with music.

O.S. Off-screen. This element of the character cue is used when a speaking character is at the exact location of the scene but not on camera.

pacing. The rhythm and speed at which the script is read.

parenthetical. Instructions that appear in the character cue that appears in parentheses. This shows how the actor should deliver the spoken line.

plot holes. An error in the script that misses a plot point is needed to advance the plot logically.

plot points. Events that happen in a script that help advance the story.

plot point 2. The event that finishes the second act. This presents the point of no return and leads to the third act.

POV. Point of view. A shot that denotes what a character sees at that moment.

production script. A script that is ready to shoot. It includes information such as camera shots and other production terms.

protagonist. The main character whose actions move the story forward.

resolution. A scene after the climax that shows the protagonist in their new world.

rewrite. To write or revise a written draft to improve it.

scene. An event that occurs at one location and moment in time.

scene header. Text in all caps at the start of a scene. It describes things like location and time of day.

screenplay. A manuscript or document that presents the story for a feature or short film.

sequence. A group of scenes is linked thematically, presenting a narrative inside the main story.

story. A collection of events that, when presented together logically, can create a narrative to entertain.

subtext. The underlying or implicit meaning in dialogue, as in a literary work.

tagline. A marketing blurb that appears on a movie poster.

three-act structure. A scriptwriting structure created by Syd Field, based on Aristotle's *Poetics*.

title page. The first page of a script. This includes the title, name of the writer, and contact information.

transitions. Visual techniques that lead one scene to the next. These can help evoke an emotional response from the viewer based on the type of transition used.

treatment. A document written in prose. This tells the story of the script before the actual script is written.

V.O. Voice-over. Like an O.S., but the speaking character is not at the physical location: a phone call, a radio deejay, or a narrator.

WGA. Writers Guild of America. A labor union that protects the rights of writers.

writer's block. A condition that prevents a writer from writing. This is often caused by fear and other related factors.

SOURCES

Akers, W. M. (n.d.). *Rewrite your script: 3 angles of attack for rewriting a screenplay*. Movie Outline. Retrieved November 18, 2022, from https://www.movieoutline.com/articles/rewrite-your-script-3-angles-of-attack-for-rewriting-a-screenplay.html

August, J. (2009, February 25). *How to rewrite*. John August. Retrieved November 18, 2022, from https://johnaugust.com/2005/how-to-rewrite

Bronzite, D. (n.d.). *A glossary of screenwriting terms & filmmaking definitions*. Movie Outline. Retrieved November 18, 2022, from https://www.movieoutline.com/articles/a-glossary-of-screenwriting-terms-and-filmmaking-definitions.html

Curtis, J. C. (2014, November 4). *7 tension-building tips for writing action scenes*. Write It Sideways. Retrieved November 18, 2022, from https://writeitsideways.com/7-tension-building-tips-for-writing-action-scenes/

Dictionary.com. (n.d.). Dictionary.com. Retrieved November 18, 2022, from https://www.dictionary.com/

Dirks, T. (n.d.). *Main Film Genres*. Retrieved November 18, 2022, from https://www.filmsite.org/genres.html

Field, S. (2005). *Screenplay: The Foundations of Screenwriting*. New York, NY: Delta Trade Paperbacks.

Goins, J. (2014, October 20). *How to overcome writer's block: 14 tricks that work*. Jeff Goins. Retrieved November 18, 2022, from https://goinswriter.com/how-to-overcome-writers-block-2/

Kouguell, S. (2014, June 27). *Top five scene pacing tips: How to pace the scene*. The Script Lab. Retrieved November 18, 2022, from https://thescriptlab.com/features/screenwriting-101/2718-top-five-scene-pacing-tips-how-to-pace-the-scene/

Kuciak, M. (2012, March 26). *Pacing your script*. Script Magazine. Retrieved November 18, 2022, from https://scriptmag.com/features/pacing-your-script

Macaulay, S. (2012, May 2). *15 steps to take after you finish your script: Filmmaker Magazine*. Filmmaker Magazine. Retrieved November 18, 2022, from https://filmmakermagazine.com/45003-15-steps-to-take-after-you-finish-your-script/

Marks, C. S. (n.d.). *Five traps and tips for character development*. Retrieved November 18, 2022, from https://www.liferichpublishing.com/en/why-us/author-resources/fiction/five-traps-and-tips-for-character-development

Riley, C. (2021). *Hollywood standard: The complete and authoritative guide to script format and style*. Michael Wiese Productions.

Sarantinos, J. G. (2014, September 11). *The sequence approach to screenwriting*. Gideon's Screenwriting Tips: Now You're a Screenwriter. Retrieved November 18, 2022, from https://gideonsway.wordpress.com/2010/04/19/the-sequence-approach-to-screenwriting/

Sarantinos, J. G. (2016, April 22). *How to shorten your film script*. Gideon's Screenwriting Tips: Now You're a Screenwriter. Retrieved November 18, 2022, from https://gideonsway.wordpress.com/2012/08/08/how-to-trim-your-script/

Sarantinos, J. G. (2016, July 18). *Pacing your film script*. Gideon's Screenwriting Tips: Now You're a Screenwriter. Retrieved November 18, 2022, from https://gideonsway.wordpress.com/2012/01/08/pacing-your-script/

Schilf, M. (2010, November 27). *Character flaws: Better conflict*. The Script Lab. Retrieved November 18, 2022, from https://thescriptlab.com/screenwriting/script-tips/876-character-flaws-better-conflict/

Script Reader Pro. (2020, June 29). *How to use short film scripts to start your writing career*. Script Reader Pro. Retrieved November 18, 2022, from https://www.scriptreaderpro.com/short-movie-scripts/

Vogler, C. (2007). *The Writer's Journey: Mythic Structure for Writers*. Studio City, CA: Michael Wiese Productions.

Walther, B. (2021, January 28). *50 bad jokes that you can't help but laugh at*. Reader's Digest Canada. Retrieved November 18, 2022, from https://www.readersdigest.ca/culture/bad-jokes-cant-help-laugh-at/

Weiland, K. M. (2013, September 25). *An insanely simple trick for tightening your dialogue*. Helping Writers Become Authors. Retrieved November 18, 2022, from https://www.helpingwritersbecomeauthors.com/an-insanely-simple-trick-for-tightening/

Welcome to the U.S. Copyright Office. (n.d.). U.S. Copyright Office. Retrieved November 18, 2022, from https://copyright.gov/

Williams, S. D. (n.d.). *Writing good log lines*. Movie Outline. Retrieved November 18, 2022, from https://www.movieoutline.com/articles/writing-good-log-lines.html

Winkle, C. (2014, February 7). *The eight character archetypes of the hero's journey*. Mythcreants. Retrieved November 18, 2022, from https://mythcreants.com/blog/the-eight-character-archetypes-of-the-heros-journey/

Winslow, K. (2022, August 23). *Subject guides: The monomyth (the hero's journey): Home*. Home - The Monomyth (The Hero's Journey) - Subject Guides at. Retrieved November 18, 2022, from https://libguides.gvsu.edu/monomyth

Writers Guild of America West. (n.d.). Retrieved November 18, 2022, from https://www.wga.org/

ABOUT THE AUTHOR

Edward Santiago is a screenwriter residing in Austin, Texas, by way of Puerto Rico. His script, *The Badge, The Gun, and The Hangman's Noose*, received the 2019 Get Connected $10K short film grant. His feature script, *Knights of the Valiant Heart*, won at the 2015 Shriekfest Horror Film Fest in Los Angeles. His writing has garnered numerous accolades, including being a finalist at the prestigious Page Awards. When he's not writing, he teaches screenwriting at the Austin School of Film. He is an avid fan of horror, science fiction, and Western films.

His next work will be his first novel, *Knights of the Valiant Heart*.

Printed in the United States
by Baker & Taylor Publisher Services